The Art of Tambourine and Triangle Playing

by

Neil Grover

and

Garwood Whaley

Copyright © 1997 MEREDITH MUSIC PUBLICATIONS
International Copyright Secured   Made in U.S.A.   All Rights Reserved

Published By
MEREDITH MUSIC PUBLICATIONS
a division of G.W. Music, Inc.

MEREDITH MUSIC PUBLICATIONS and its stylized double M logo are trademarks of Meredith Music Publications, a division of G.W. Music, Inc.

Book design and layout by Shawn Brown
Cover design by John Heinly

No part of this book may be reproduced or transmitted in any form or by any means, electronic or mechanical, including photocopying, recording or by any informational storage or retrieval system without permission in writing from the publisher.

ISBN: 1-57463-050-4

Copyright © 1997 MEREDITH MUSIC PUBLICATIONS
International Copyright Secured   Made in U.S.A.   All Rights Reserved

First Edition
September 1997

CONTENTS

INTRODUCTION 4

SELECTED LITERATURE 5

ABOUT THE TAMBOURINE 6

TAMBOURINE EXERCISES
    One Hand Studies 8
    Shake Rolls 10
    Thumb Rolls 12
    Fist-Knee 14
    Fingers on Rim 16
    Grace Notes 18
    Right Hand Shake Roll 19
    Multiple Techniques with Dynamics 20
    Duet 22

ABOUT THE TRIANGLE 23

TRIANGLE EXERCISES
    One Hand Strokes 25
        with Rests (muffling) 27
        with Sixteenth Notes 29
        with Rests (muffling) 30
    Rolls 31
    Fast Articulations 34
    Multiple Techniques with Dynamics 36
    Grace Notes 38
    Duet 39

ABOUT THE AUTHORS 40

INTRODUCTION

The tambourine and triangle are two of the most ignored instruments in the percussion family. While most serious percussion students spend time practicing snare drum, timpani and keyboard percussion, few spend time practicing accessory instruments like tambourine and triangle. This is unfortunate since both student and professional percussionists spend much of their performance time playing on accessory instruments.

Percussion instruments, especially tambourine and triangle, require separate and unique techniques that are difficult to master and cannot be learned "on the job." Like any musical instrument, skillful playing can only be achieved through study and practice.

This text provides information on the history, selection and fundamental performance techniques for both tambourine and triangle. It also provides skill-development exercises and duets that cover all of the essential performance techniques for both instruments. The list of selected literature provides outstanding examples of the use of these instruments in both band and orchestra. We would like to thank Dr. Guy Gauthreaux for his assistance in compiling this list and Frank Kumiega for his assistance with the diagrams.

It is our belief that an artistic approach to tambourine and triangle playing will result from the careful study and diligent practice of the materials contained in this text.

—*Neil Grover and Garwood Whaley*

SELECTED LITERATURE

The following works represent excellent writing for tambourine and triangle and present technical and/or musical challenges for both instruments. The study and performance of these works will allow the percussionist to apply the techniques presented in this book to works in the band and orchestra repertoire.

BAND/WIND ENSEMBLE   ORCHESTRA

Tambourine

Armenian Dances	Reed	*Arabian Dance* (Nutcracker)	Tchaikovsky
Celebration Overture	Creston	*Carmen*	Bizet
Fiesta Del Pacifico	Nixon	*Carnaval Overture*	Dvorak
Festival Variations	Smith	*Capriccio Italien*	Tchaikovsky
Incantation and Dance	Chance	*Petrouchka*	Stravinsky
Laude	Hanson	*Polovetzian Dances*	Borodin
Sante Fe Saga	Gould	*Rhapsodie Espagnol*	Ravel
Symphony in Bb	Hindemith	*Roman Carnival Overture*	Berlioz
Putza	Van Der Roost	*Scheherazade*	Rimsky-Korsakov
Variations On America	Ives	*Trepak* (Nutcracker)	Tchaikovsky

Triangle

Armenian Dances	Reed	*Abduction From The Seraglio* Overture	Mozart
First Suite in Eb for Military Band	Holst	*Carmen*	Bizet
March of The Belgian Paratroopers	Leemans	*Capriccio Espagnol*	Rimsky-Korsakov
Music for Prague	Husa	*Hungarian Dance no. 5*	Dvorak
Original Suite for Military Band	Jacob	*New World Symphony*	Dvorak
Sea Treaders	McBeth	*Piano Concerto no. 1*	Liszt
Toccatta Marziale	Vaughn Williams	*Roman Carnival Overture*	Berlioz
William Byrd Suite	Jacob	*Scheherazade*	Rimsky-Korsakov
Variations On America	Ives	*Symphony no. 4*	Brahms
Variations on a Theme of Robert Schumann	Jager	*Symphony no. 3*	Mahler

ABOUT THE TAMBOURINE

English	Tambourine
German	die Shellentrommel, das tamburin
Italian	il tamburello (basco), il tamburino, il tamburo basco
French	le tambour de basque
Spanish	la pandereta

HISTORY

The tambourine is a frame drum usually made of a wooden shell or hoop and a head of calfskin. The wood shell contains small openings around the shell in which pairs of metal disc shaped jingles are loosely attached. Tambourines normally have one or two rows of jingles made from a variety of metals such as brass or copper. This combination of head and jingles uniquely qualifies the instrument as both an idiophone and a membranophone. Although tambourines may vary in size from quite small to very large, most orchestral and concert band instruments are between 10 and 12 inches in diameter.

The tambourine is an ancient percussion instrument with references being made in the Old Testament and pictured in art works of the Romans. During the late middle ages and early Renaissance, it was popular with jugglers and wandering musicians. According to Karl Geiringer, "The instrument was not merely struck with the hand, but was also thrown up into the air and caught again."[1] Its popularity as a dance and folk instrument in Spain and Italy was probably due to the fact that it was the instrument of gypsies. The tambourine was of little importance during the Baroque period, however, its importance began to emerge during the Classical period. " Around the year 1800 it gained a firm place in the Janissary music which the European military bands had taken over from the Turks, and soon thereafter it also appeared in the Classical orchestra where it was used to underline folk and dance elements."[2]

Standard performance techniques include striking the instrument with braced fingers, flat hand, fist or knee and producing sustained sounds by playing shake or thumb rolls. Contemporary composers call for special effects by playing with a variety of sticks, mallets and beaters, playing on multiple tambourines and actually dropping the instrument on the floor.

SELECTION

When selecting a tambourine, the most important factor is the type and quality of jingles. A fine quality tambourine will have jingles that are capable of responding at all dynamic levels and producing a clear articulation. There are many types of jingles available made from a variety of metal alloys and manufactured by stamping or hammering. In addition to jingles, the instrument should have a good quality head securely mounted to a solid, hardwood frame. A tight head provides a playing surface capable of quick response and clear articulation.

PERFORMANCE

Holding the instrument properly is the first step in developing acceptable performance technique. A good tambourine will have a grip area usually with a hole for mounting the instrument on a stand when playing multiple-percussion parts. Although the mounting hole is sometimes referred to as the

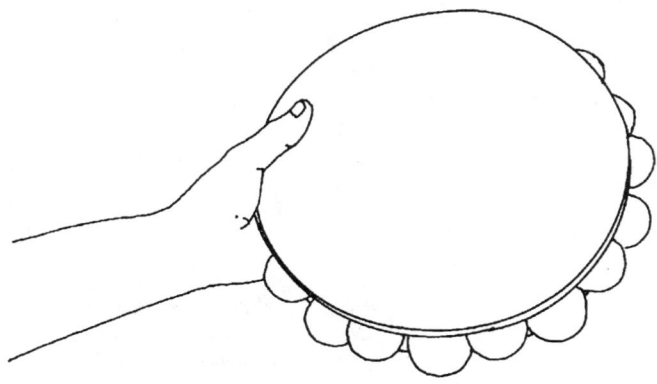

"thumb hole," it is not intending for finger placement. Grip the tambourine firmly but not too tight since it must be free to vibrate when struck. Holding the instrument too tightly will inhibit the jingles from moving and consequently choke the sound.

With the hand striking the tambourine, bunch all five fingers together to form a striking surface. Use this "finger pad" to strike the instrument a third of the way in from the edge. This spot will produce the best balance between head and jingle sounds. When playing softly, play near the edge. For louder dynamics, move toward the center. It is important to experiment to find the best playing area for each individual instrument.

Begin playing with the tambourine held parallel to the floor (horizontal orientation) striking the instrument slowly. As you play, slowly angle the tambourine up until it is perpendicular to the floor (vertical orientation). You'll notice that the sonority of the tambourine has changed from "dry" to "wet." Changes in orientation can be used to enhance articulation or jingle resonance. For most playing situations, the tambourine should be held at an orientation half way between horizontal and vertical.

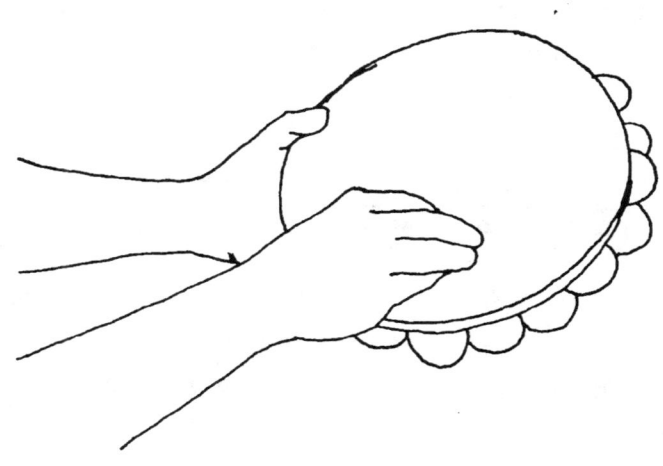

---

[1] Geiringer, Karl. Musical Instruments. London: George Allen & Unwin Ltd, 1965.
[2] Peinkofer, Karl and Tannigel, Fritz. Handbook of Percussion Instruments. Mainz, Germany: Schott, 1969.

ONE HAND STUDIES

Play this exercise with one hand holding the tambourine firmly but do not restrict its motion. Play the exercise three ways as follows:

1) *piano*, using thumb, pointer and index fingers playing on the edge.
2) *mezzo forte*, adding ring finger and playing half way between the edge and center.
3) *forte*, with fist in the center of the head.

Strive to insure that all rhythms are crystal clear with no extraneous jingle sound. Your performance starts before you pick up the instrument and ends after you put it down!

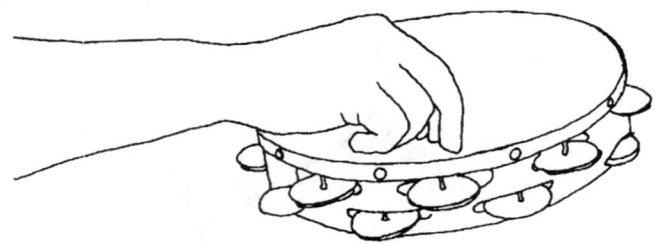

This is another one-handed study but utilizes rhythms that are characteristic of those found in a typical tambourine part. Play the rhythms as precise and rhythmically articulate as possible. Remember to hold the tambourine firmly in a horizontal orientation and strike using a relaxed motion. As in the previous study, use different dynamic levels.

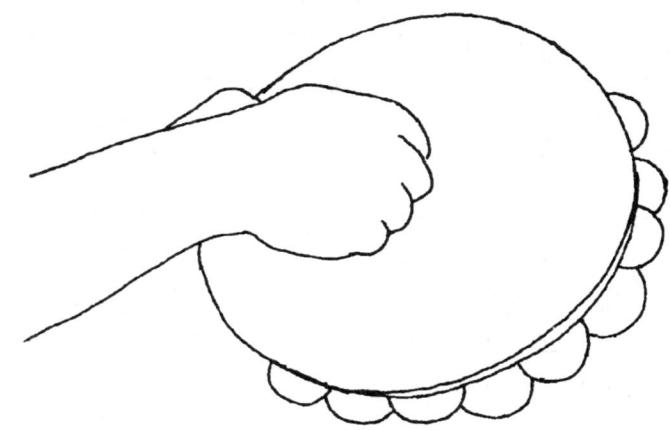

SHAKE ROLLS

This study emphasizes shake rolls. Note that each roll contains an attack, a sustain and a release. To properly execute a smooth shake roll, make sure that the instrument is held in a vertical orientation; the jingles must vibrate on the pin and have room to move and resonate. When playing a shake roll, the wrist and arm must remain relaxed. To insure a clean attack and release, begin and end each shake roll with an unaccented stroke.

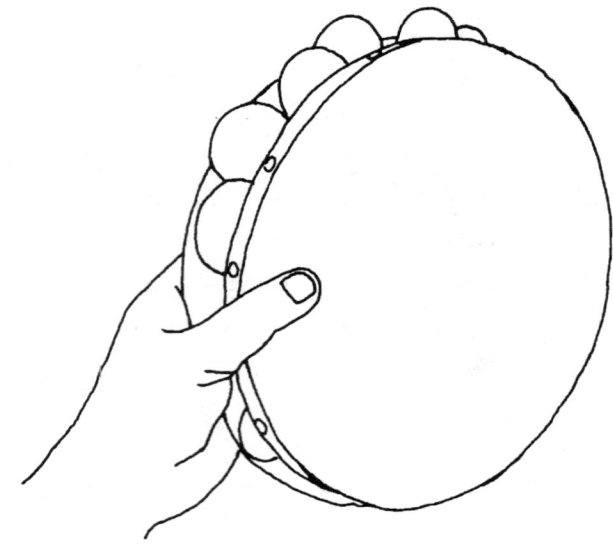

Soft shake rolls are difficult to play. Practice this study at all dynamic levels, especially soft. Vibrate the instrument as fast as possible to insure a smooth, consistent roll. When playing soft shake rolls, minimize the side-to-side motion; use a slight vibration of the hand only. The louder the roll, the larger the shaking motion. Be patient, developing the muscles used in playing shake rolls will take time and practice.

THUMB ROLLS

This study introduces thumb rolls which are executed by rubbing the thumb of the striking hand around the circumference of the tambourine head. The following will help:

- Bend your thumb back as far as is comfortable.
- Make sure that your thumb points in the direction of movement (think of your thumb as a car always pointed in a forward motion).
- Using the fleshy part of the thumb, apply a light yet consistent pressure against the head-do not push too hard.
- Moisten your thumb with your tongue in order to create friction between your thumb and the head. Friction is the necessary component for playing a thumb roll.

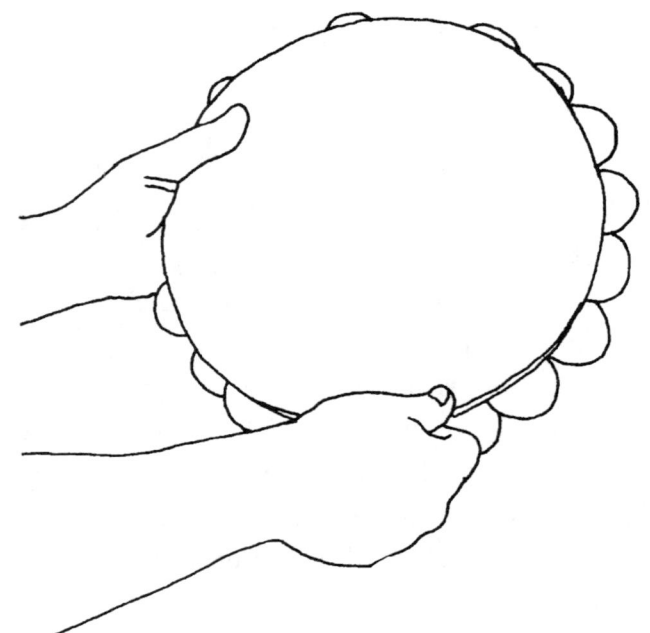

When playing a thumb roll, imagine a clock face. Place your thumb at the 6 o'clock position and smoothly and lightly rub your thumb counter clockwise around the outer circumference of the tambourine head. Try again! Although it may take several attempts, once achieved, a thumb roll is not difficult to repeat.

FIST/KNEE

The fist/knee technique is used when executing rapid articulations. While standing, elevate your leg by placing your foot on a stool or chair (your elevated thigh should be approximately parallel to the floor). If you hold the tambourine in your left hand, use your right knee and vice versa. Hold the tambourine upside down with the head facing the floor. Create a "sandwich" of knee, 6 inches of air, tambourine, 6 inches of air and then your fist. Keeping the knee and fist stationary, make an up and down motion using the arm to alternate the tambourine between hitting your fist and your knee. All motion is controlled with the arm, not the wrist. This technique is the only time you should grip the tambourine very firmly while keeping a stiff wrist.

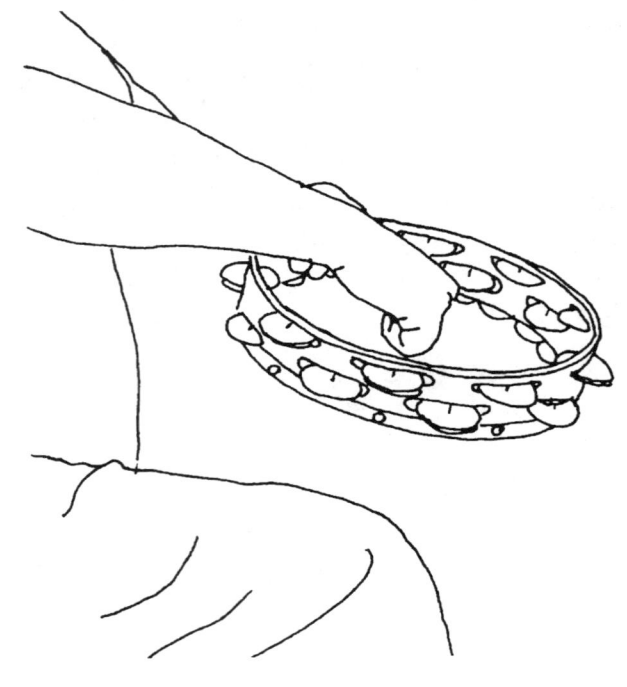

When using the fist/knee technique, play as much as possible using only the fist saving the fist/knee technique for passages too fast to be played with one hand. In this study, the knee should not be used until measure 3. Work on rhythmic accuracy and clean articulation. Play this study at various dynamic levels attempting to achieve a good flow of the instrument between knee and fist. The softer the dynamic level, the more difficult it is to execute clean, even articulations.

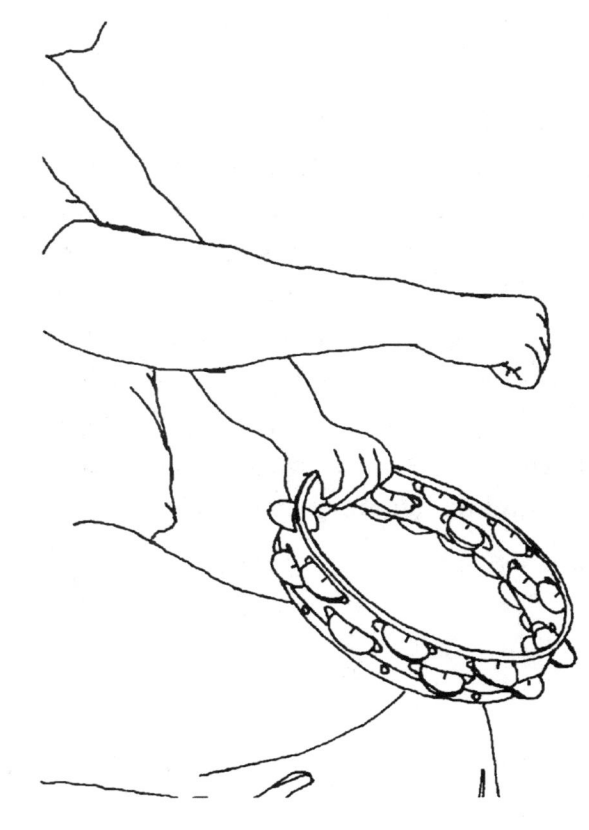

FINGERS ON RIM

This exercise is to be played using a one hand—two finger technique. Hold the tambourine normally and strike the instrument using the pointer and index fingers from the opposite hand. When first attempting this technique, you will notice that the playing fingers do not produce an equal sound; one finger will probably sound stronger. The goal of this study is to produce even sounds throughout with both fingers sounding dynamically equal.

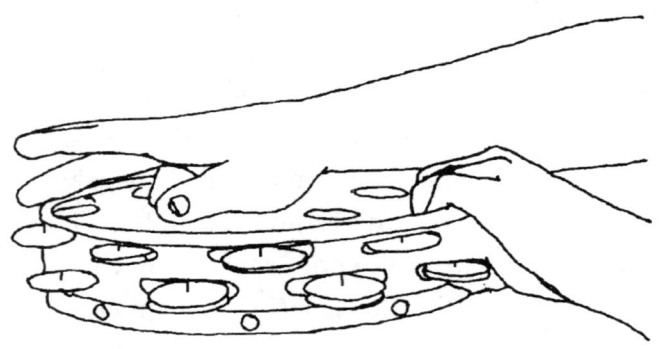

Although similar to the previous study, this exercise is executed using a different technique. While standing, place your foot on a chair to elevate your leg and knee (similar to fist/knee technique). Rest the tambourine, upside down, on the thigh of the elevated leg. The tambourine should be fairly flat and balanced on the thigh. Rest the fingers of both hands on the tambourine rim farthest away from you. Bring your forearms down until they rest against the rim area closest to you. Using the forearms to brace the tambourine against the thigh, use the combined pointer and index fingers from each hand to play. Although awkward at first, this is an often used and valuable technique.

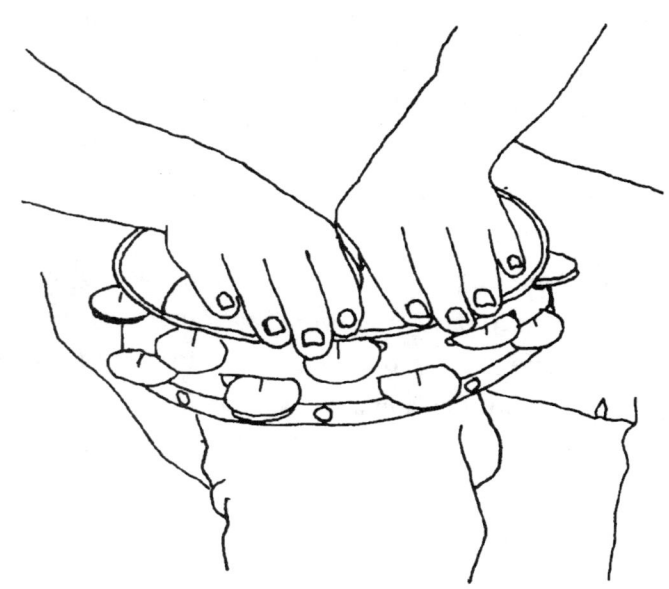

GRACE NOTES

While not commonly found in tambourine parts, grace notes do occasionally appear and can be problematic. Play this study holding the tambourine in the same manner as described on page 17. Grace notes are played with a concept similar to that used on snare drum. Play all ruffs using the index finger and then the pointer finger from one hand, then play the main note with the fingers of the opposite hand. Flams are played using the pointer finger from one hand for the grace note and the fingers from the opposite hand for the main note.

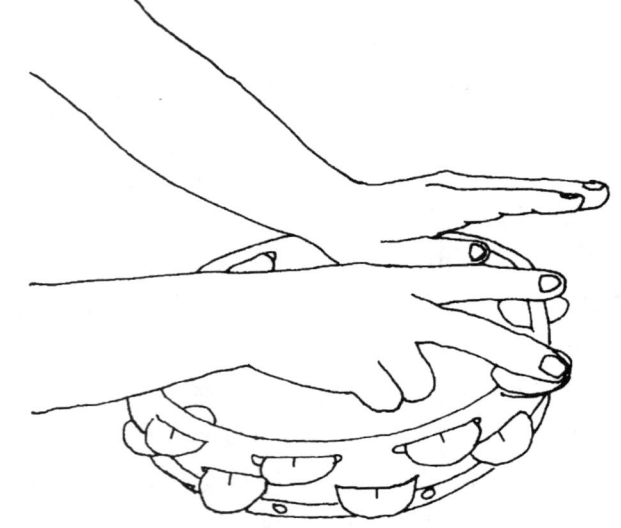

Not too fast

mp

RIGHT HAND SHAKE ROLL

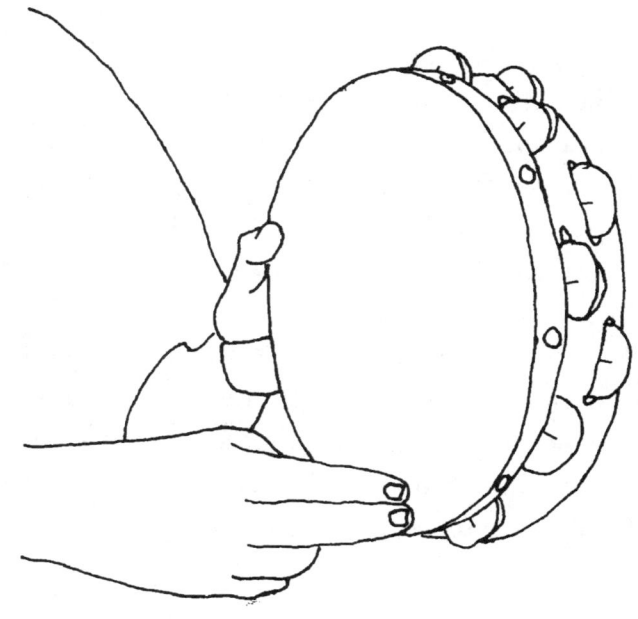

This study introduces the right hand shake technique, useful for starting or playing soft shake rolls. Hold the tambourine in the left hand in a vertical orientation and place the index and pointer fingers from the right hand on the bottom edge of the head. It is important to relax and hold the tambourine loosely; it must be free to vibrate. Using only the fingers from the right hand, vibrate the tambourine very quickly and softly. At first the motion is created only with the fingers. Slowly vibrate harder and let the left hand take over in a normal shake roll. Practice this method of playing very soft, long shake rolls using only the fingers as well as rolls which crescendo. When you have mastered this technique try the reverse (start a normal loud shake roll, decrescendo and switch to a right hand shake roll). The transition from normal shake roll to right hand finger roll is difficult and requires much practice.

MULTIPLE TECHNIQUES WITH DYNAMICS

This difficult exercise uses thumb rolls and knee/fist techniques. In order to switch from one technique to another, time has been left in measures four and thirteen. Begin this study with the tambourine held in one hand, switching to the fist/knee technique in measure four. Switch back again during measure thirteen. The long roll in measures twenty and twenty-one can employ the right hand shake roll if needed. Try to minimize excess jingle sounds during the shifts, making sure to count carefully and enter on the correct beat.

Begin this study with the tambourine resting on your thigh and playing with a two-hand technique. Switch to fist/knee technique in measure eight (the tambourine should still be upside down). Attack the roll in measure fifteen with your fist and play a normal shake roll. Come out of the roll playing in the normal manner.

TAMBOURINE DUET

ABOUT THE TRIANGLE

English	Triangle
German	der Triangel
Italian	il triangolo
French	le triangle
Spanish	el triangulo

HISTORY

The triangle is rarely viewed as a musical instrument that requires serious practice and study. Nothing could be farther from the truth. The tonal texture of a triangle is that of a special nature which cannot be imitated. The instrument was used as early as the Turks with their Janissary music and eventually found its way into the classical orchestra repertoire of the eighteenth, nineteenth and twentieth centuries. "The triangle entered the European orchestra in the 18th century by way of the Janissary music of the Turkish soldiers."[1] Drawings of early instruments show rings loosely hung which provided additional sound when struck. According to James Blades, " The humble triangle can lay claim to being one of the first purely metal percussion instruments to enter the modern orchestra (Hamburg Opera 1710). Until the end of the eighteenth century. . .it was used mainly to give added color. It became a permanent member of the orchestra during the early part of the following century, and in 1853 was raised to the rank of a symphonic solo instrument by Liszt in his Piano Concerto in E flat, causing, it is said, considerable consternation."[2] Early examples of triangles include ornamental work at the open end, often in a scroll pattern.

Historically, the triangle has been manufactured from a solid iron and later steel rod and bent into a triangular shape roughly equilateral. In modern times, the scroll pattern has been abandoned and triangles are made from either steel or brass. Just after the turn of the century in the United States, triangles were fashioned in New England using the spindle from knitting machines (during this period, New England was the regional center for knitting mills). These spindles were fabricated from hardened steel which was turned on a metal lathe. The result was a triangle with sides of unequal diameter.

Most triangles range in size from four to ten inches in diameter. The preferred size for orchestra and concert band is between six and nine inches, the larger size being more suitable for literature from the Romantic period. Since there is no "correct" triangle size, it is the responsibility of the percussionist to select an instrument of suitable sonority for each particular work. Although the triangle is of indefinite pitch, it tends to blend with the overall harmonic sound of the band and orchestra.

ACCESSORIES

The manner in which the triangle is suspended is critical to the quality of sound produced. Since the triangle is a highly resonant instrument and must be free to vibrate, a good triangle clip with a very thin suspension line is essential. A suspension line that is too thick or heavy will prevent the triangle from vibrating and produce an undesirable sound. One of the best materials to use is monofilament fishing line which is readily available and inexpensive. When tying the line to the clip, do not leave much slack or the triangle will have a tendency to turn when played. Make a second "safety" loop larger than the primary loop in case the first loop breaks.

The size and weight of the beater is also of great importance. Generally, heavier beaters of various metals produce the most sonorous sounds. There are a variety of beaters on the market today that are suitable for all types of music and ensembles.

PERFORMANCE

Hold the triangle in the weaker of the two hands. The clip should be held between the ring finger and the thumb with the pointer on top. This method leaves the other fingers free for muffling. If at all

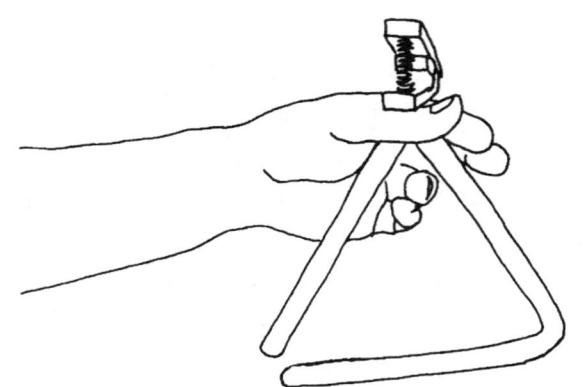

possible, play the triangle with one hand while suspending it with the other. By holding the instrument up the sound is more easily projected and there are no extraneous stand sounds.

Strike the triangle "pushing out" away from the body while holding the instrument at eye level. When struck properly, the triangle will produce a fundamental sound with numerous overtones. The production of overtones is important and enables the instrument to blend with an ensemble. The triangle is a "coloration" instrument and must always blend with the ensemble. The instrument may be struck on the bottom or on the side. Wherever the instrument is struck, it must be with a pushing motion since a slapping motion will produce a hard, metallic ping rather than a beautiful, resonant tone.

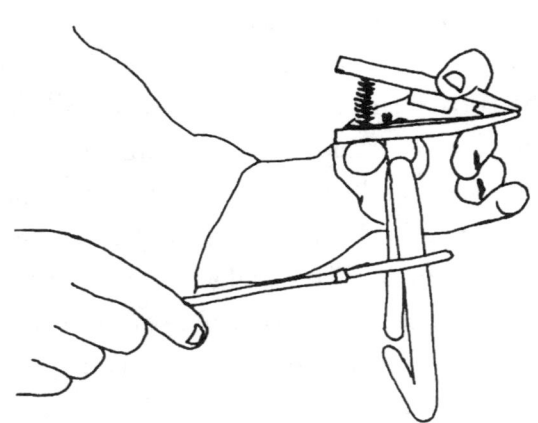
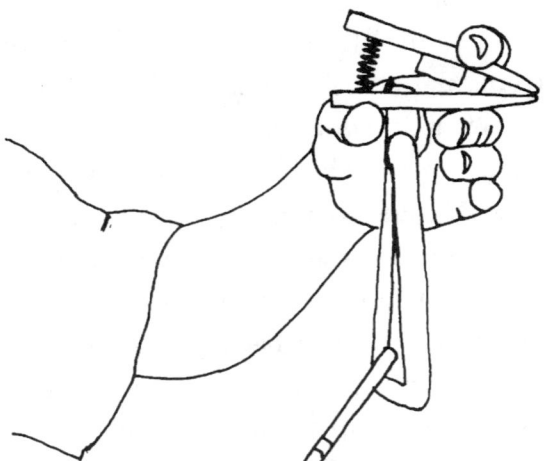

Standard performance techniques include striking the instrument with steel beaters and, for special effects, wooden sticks. Fast rhythms are played either by suspending the triangle and using one beater in each hand or by moving a single beater back and forth from side to side on the inside of the instrument.

---

1 Peinkofer, Karl and Tannigel, Fritz. Handbook of Percussion Instruments. Mainz, Germany:Schott, 1969.
2 Blades, James. Percussion Instruments and Their History. London, Faber and Faber Limited, 1970.

ONE-HAND STROKES

While playing this exercise, concentrate on holding the triangle properly and producing a full, rich sound. Remember, a good triangle sound consists of a fundamental pitch and its overtones. Experiment with different playing areas to find a "sweet spot" which produces the maximum overtone resonance and "shimmer."

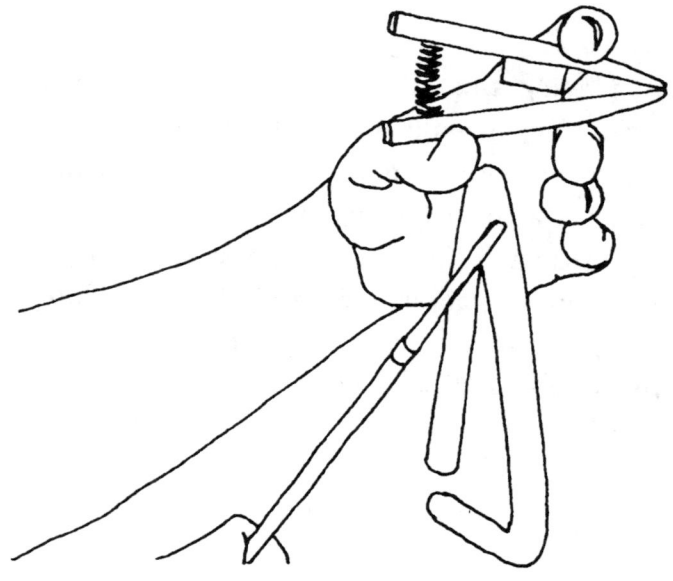

ONE-HAND STROKES

Try playing this study at a moderately fast tempo. You should be able to execute all rhythms cleanly and evenly with one hand. Maintain a consistent dynamic level and tone color. Although the overall effect may be somewhat "ringy," you should be able to articulate clearly and bring out the rhythmic pulse. Play this exercise at different dynamic levels.

ONE-HAND STROKES WITH MUFFLING

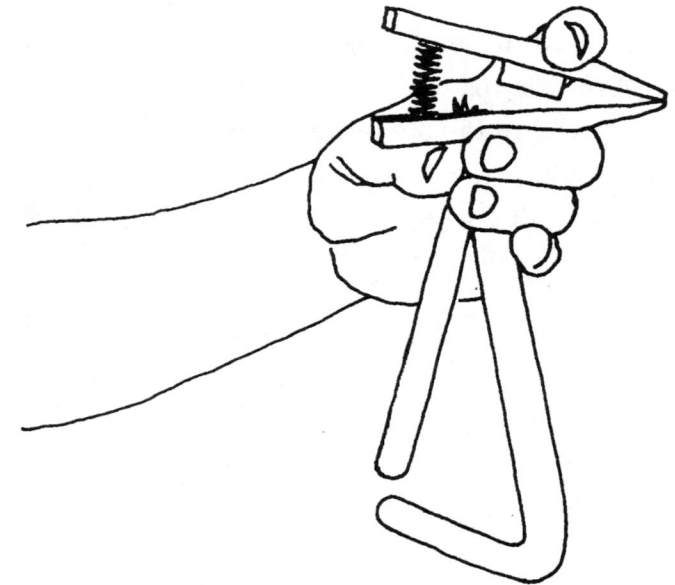

This exercise introduces the concept of muffling which is accomplished using the free fingers of the hand supporting the triangle clip. Simply touch one, two or three fingers to the triangle to dampen the sound. Dampening is a useful technique used to eliminate extraneous ringing of the instrument. While playing this etude, muffle during all rests. However, when playing actual triangle parts, be careful not to over muffle. Remember, the triangle produces a sound-coloring-texture which is meant to ring.

ONE-HAND STROKES WITH MUFFLING

This muffling etude uses both quarter note and eighth note rests which should each be muffled. Be attentive to note duration to insure that all note values remain consistent. Give each note its full value being careful not to cut notes off (muffle) prematurely.

ONE-HAND STROKES—FAST

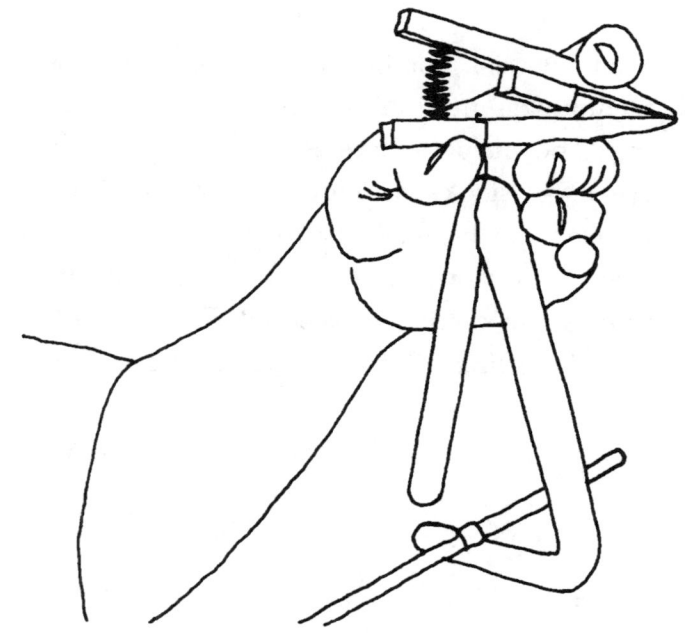

Fast rhythmic passages are executed by striking the triangle from the inside on either the side and bottom or the two sides. This technique requires quite a bit of practice but, once mastered, is invaluable. Make sure that the "up" stroke or the "side" stroke (depending on which technique you use) is properly timed for rhythmic accuracy. To develop this technique, practice playing even eighth or sixteenth notes. This etude is difficult to play evenly and should be practiced slowly at first before increasing tempo.

Not too fast

ONE-HAND STROKES WITH MUFFLING

This exercise combines two previously used techniques; muffling and two-sided-inner playing. The purpose here is to develop an even, two-sided-stroke technique. Adding muffling increases the level of difficulty. Again, practice this study slowly making sure that the techniques are correctly executed. With time, triangle muffling will become automatic.

ROLLS

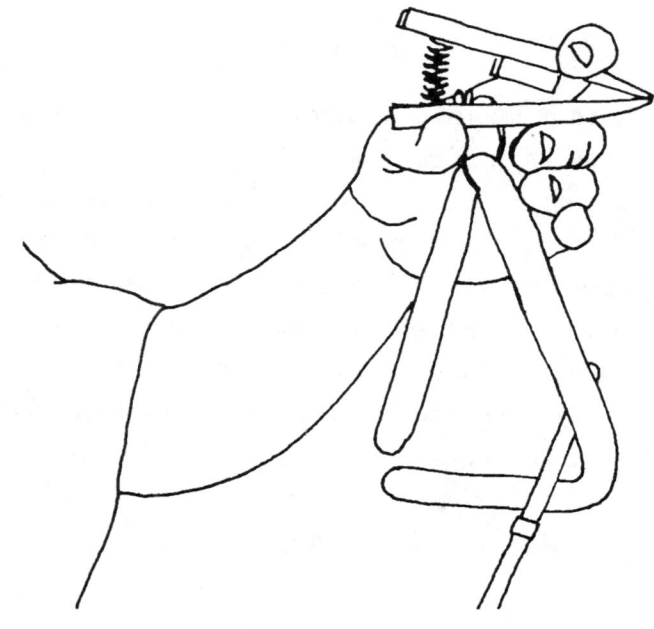

The ability to play a good triangle roll takes both practice and patience. Rolls are played on two (not three) sides of the instrument and in general, the faster they are played, the smoother they sound. Play soft rolls with the tip of the beater in the extreme corner of the instrument. Loud rolls are played about one third of the way down the beater length and close to the middle of the two sides. Practice rolls at all dynamic levels including loud to soft and soft to loud.

ROLLS

Here is another etude that focuses on triangle rolls. The difficulty with this study is execution of quarter note rolls. Much the same way that a snare drummer practices five, seven and nine stroke rolls, the triangle player must practice short rolls. Try playing this exercise at a moderate to fast tempo. Be sure that each quarter note roll is exactly the same duration and contains the same number of strokes. To insure a consistent concluding sound, end each roll on the same side of the triangle.

THE ART OF TAMBOURINE AND TRIANGLE PLAYING / 33

This exercise introduces the short eighth note roll. As previously mentioned, short triangle rolls require diligent practice. Play this study as follows. First, at a tempo that allows eighth note rolls to be played as nine - stroke rolls. Second, at a tempo that allows eighth note rolls to be played as seven-stroke rolls. And third, at a tempo that allows eighth note rolls to be played as five-stroke rolls.

FAST ARTICULATIONS

It is sometimes necessary to use two beaters to play very fast rhythmic articulations. This technique requires the triangle to be suspended on a clip from either a music stand or from a stand built specially for triangle. Although this method compromises sound quality, it is necessary at times. In order to minimize sound transmission to the music stand, apply felt or moleskin to the triangle clip.

Moderately Fast

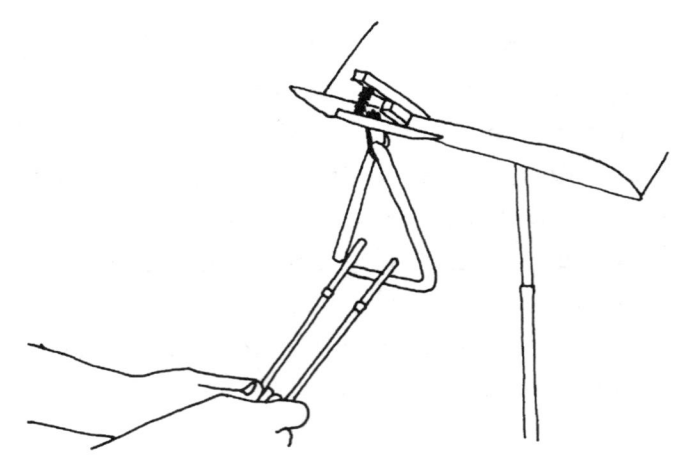

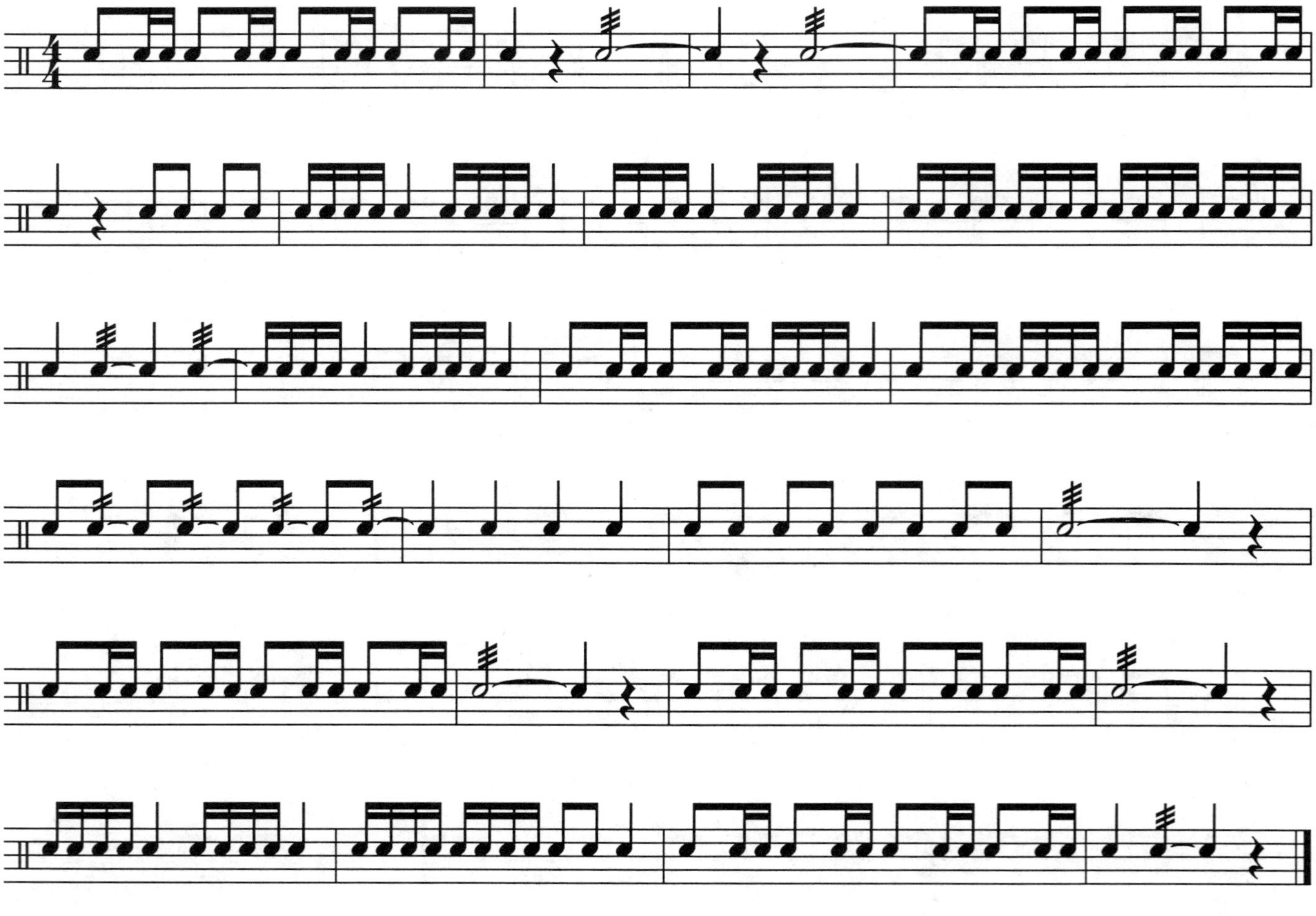

This study, similar to the previous one, requires muffling during the short eighth note/ eighth rest passages. Muffle gently so as not to cause the triangle to spin. Practice this technique by playing a series of short strokes followed by a gentle, yet complete dampening of sound. Incorporate this technique into the exercise so that the muffling does not interfere with rhythmic accuracy.

MULTIPLE TECHNIQUES WITH DYNAMICS

Practice this exercise two ways. Play with one hand at a "not too fast" tempo which will require quick yet subtle movement when going from rolls to single notes. Also, practice at a faster tempo with the triangle suspended using two beaters. Since this technique can compromise sound quality, listen carefully and try to achieve a rich, full sound.

Again, practice this exercise two ways; "not too fast" using one beater and faster with the triangle suspended and using two beaters. The sudden dynamic changes from loud to soft may require subtle muffling to stop the natural ring of the instrument. Practice this technique out of context and with various dynamic combinations. By softly touching the instrument with one or two fingers, the instruments ring can be reduced or totally removed. This is an important technique which should be practiced until complete control is acquired.

GRACE NOTES

Playing grace notes on triangle is always challenging. This study can be played using two beaters on a suspended triangle or by using a one hand technique. Practice both ways. When playing with one hand, keep the beater close to a corner and use alternate strokes. Begin all grace notes before the beat and play them with less emphasis than the main note. Practice this technique slowly at first playing all grace notes "open." Gradually increase speed and close up the grace notes. The grace note sound is similar to snare drum except that the triangle will ring through articulations.

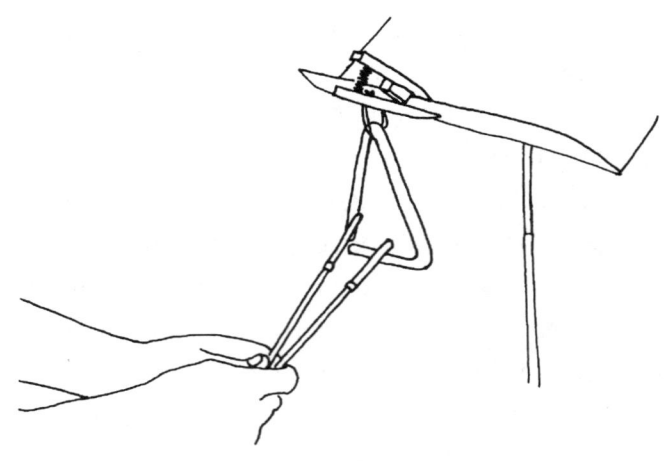

TRIANGLE DUET

ABOUT THE AUTHORS

Neil Grover is a world-renowned cymbal, tambourine and triangle specialist. For the past twenty years, he has performed with the Boston Symphony and Boston Pops. Additional credentials include performances with the Royal Ballet of England, Boston Musica Viva, American Ballet Theatre, Bolshoi Ballet and Boston Symphony Chamber Players.

Neil Grover has been a featured clinician at the Percussive Arts Society International Conventions, Texas Music Educators Association Convention, New Jersey State Percussion Ensemble Festival, University of Miami, North Texas State University, Berklee College, University of Nevada, Interlochen Arts Academy, Iowa PAS Day of Percussion, Northwestern University, North Dakota Day of Percussion, University of Massachusetts, University of Texas, Indiana University, Oberlin College and the First International Percussion Festival of Puerto Rico. In addition, he has been the subject of feature articles in *Percussive Notes, Modern Drummer, Drum Tracks*, and *Musical Merchandise Review*.

As founder and president of Grover Pro Percussion, Inc., Neil Grover's innovative designs and manufacturing techniques have catapulted the standards of excellence in the percussion industry. Neil was formerly an adjunct professor of music at the Boston Conservatory and the University of Massachusetts. Neil holds the distinction of serving on both the Board of Directors and the Sustaining Members Advisory Council of the Percussive Arts Society.

Garwood Whaley was educated at the Juilliard School of Music and at The Catholic University of America where he earned the Doctor of Musical Arts Degree. While completing graduate work, he performed for six years with The United States Army Band in Washington, D.C. Dr. Whaley has been the recipient of the *Outstanding Secondary Educators of America Award, Outstanding National Catholic Bandmaster*, The National Band Association's *Citation of Excellence*, The National Federation Interscholastic Music Association *Outstanding Music Educator Award*, The 1994 *Alumni Achievement Award* in the field of Education from The Catholic University of America, the John Philip Sousa Foundation's *Legion of Honor* award and has been included in Who's Who in American Music and the International Who's Who in Music.

Dr. Whaley is an Adjunct Professor of Music at The Catholic University of America, President of Meredith Music Publications, Curriculum Coordinator of Instrumental Music for the Diocese of Arlington (VA) Schools, Director of the nationally acclaimed Bishop Ireton Symphonic Wind Ensemble, Chief Editor for Music for Percussion, Inc., and Past President of the Percussive Arts Society.

Whaley has performed as conductor, adjudicator and clinician throughout the United States including The Mid-West International Band and Orchestra Clinic, Texas Music Educators Association Convention, Texas Bandmasters Convention, Wisconsin Music Educators Association Convention, New York State School Music Association Convention, Pennsylvania Music Educators Association Convention and is a popular lecturer for university music education programs and school in-service workshops.

In addition, he has been extensively involved in music publishing. He is the author of more than twenty highly acclaimed method books for percussion instruments, two supplementary band methods (co-author), solos and ensembles and articles for various music journals.